The Art of Hospitality

The Art of Hospitality

Introduction by Pilar Guzmán
Paintings by Ignasi Monreal

ASSOULINE

PRINTEMPS
ETE

AUTOMNE
HIVER

“And now here is my secret, a very simple secret: It is only with the heart that one can see rightly; what is essential is invisible to the eye.”

Antoine de Saint-Exupéry, *The Little Prince*

I have often said that I can tell within the first few moments of entering a hotel whether the staff is happy. As the editor of a travel publication and a lifelong traveler, I've logged countless short- and long-term hotel stays, from the grand dame overlooking a famous square to the mom-and-pop motor lodge whose exterior hallway shines a fluorescent path to a lowly ice machine. Although this book celebrates the art of hospitality in its highest form, I mention the full spectrum very deliberately. Luxury service at its core has nothing to do with gold leaf, thread count, state-of-the-art spa facilities, welcome drinks, or Michelin stars. All these bells and whistles are table stakes, signifiers of luxury in today's high-end hospitality arms race. True luxury has everything, however, to do with people.

So while the lovable Ralph Fiennes character in *The Grand Budapest Hotel* satirizes the role of general manager, the film

The Four Seasons logo brought to vibrant life.

Previous pages: Classical statues depicting the four seasons, inspired by real works on the Paris and Saint Petersburg properties, capture the elegance and charm found at each hotel.

"So much of long-term success is based on intangibles. Beliefs and ideas. Invisible concepts."

Isadore Sharp, founder and chairman

Isadore Sharp, the larger-than-life personality known to many as "Issy," founded Four Seasons in 1960 and opened its first property, a 125-room motor hotel, in Toronto, Canada, the following year.

PLEASE
DO NOT
DISTURB

doesn't exaggerate the gamut of responsibilities. For M. Gustave, a day's work includes playing florist and valet in one breath and consigliere and even lover in the next, and fact isn't far from fiction. In some ways, the role of a good hotelier requires all the intimacy of a family member on the one hand as well as the discretion of a secret service agent on the other. Those of us who travel for a living can smell a fake. We have, in our mental database, a sampling of hundreds of doorman and desk clerk greetings, room service deliveries, turn-down service ministrations, and impossible eleventh-hour dinner reservations scored by a plugged-in concierge as reference. All are functions performed by (often invisible) human hands.

But while a hotel prioritizes the satisfaction of its guests above all, it trades on a much broader and more elusive ecosystem of overall human happiness: that least quantifiable yet most coveted "vibe," which no big-name designer or bar concept can achieve for any amount of money without an engaged staff who loves what they do. Sure, if the customer isn't happy, the manager isn't happy, and if the manager isn't happy—well, you know what happens next. More critical, perhaps, is the reverse logic: An unhappy staff all but guarantees an unhappy guest. Or, as Four Seasons founder and chairman Isadore Sharp says, "It's the Golden Rule—the simple idea that if you treat people well, the way you would like to be treated, they will do the same." Those successful hoteliers understand that you can't just get some of it right. Hotel happiness, in fact, depends perhaps more on the five hundred little things you don't see—which are performed by countless loyal staff you don't see—than on those twenty-five you do.

The longer you talk to a good hotelier, the more evident it becomes that hospitality is a vocation—a calling, in the truest sense of the word, that's more akin to the Marine Corps or the clergy than anything. As Patrizio Cipollini, the general manager of Four Seasons Hotel Firenze and recipient of the Best of the Best Hotelier of the Year 2018 award, says, "You hire for character and attitude and the skills follow." According to John O'Sullivan, the general manager of Four Seasons Resort Punta Mita, there is no rule book for creating a culture and responding to an existing one in certain industries. "People, including managers, don't start out being their best, necessarily," he says, "but if you hire good people and build an environment of zero blame but great accountability, you allow them to grow into being themselves in a role, which is the ultimate goal." O'Sullivan also emphasizes the importance of having fun. "We aren't putting people on the moon," he says. "We are trying to give people an amazing experience steeped in culture and in rituals unique to each place."

Comfort is paramount; with the legendary trademark
Four Seasons bed, staying at any property is nothing if not dreamlike.

Following pages: (left) Every guest is treated like royalty no matter their lineage.
(right) Four Seasons service goes above and into the deep blue beyond.

"We are constantly looking for moments to 'wow' our guests, in subtle or grand ways, and we use technology in ways that enhance the guest experience without sacrificing the human touch."

Dickson Cheng, guest services manager

Receptionists are always prepared to greet guests with a smile, even when multitasking.

Opposite: Say one word to a concierge and his expert mind is already abuzz, finding the ideal restaurant or entertainment to delight each guest. High touch, high tech.

Four
Seasons
Clefs d'Or
Search...

It also becomes obvious that joy is contagious. "I've hugged twenty-three people since I walked in this morning," O'Sullivan says of his unorthodox approach. "That's the spirit in Mexico." While waitstaff can be trained to refill a glass when it has been depleted by two thirds, character or emotional intelligence can't be mandated. When Hurricane Patricia hit Mexico a few years back, the hotel was full, but because of the emergency state, staff were advised to stay at home. "We needed help at the resort, and 140 staff showed up even though they were advised not to," O'Sullivan recalls. "They left their homes in a much less prepared state and came to work as warriors."

When artist Ignasi Monreal was commissioned by Four Seasons Hotels and Resorts to illustrate, through a series of 125 paintings, the company's celebrated service ethos, it didn't take long for him to get his inspiration. "It is the latent visible perfection that's just there that you take for granted," says Monreal, who is well-known in the art and fashion world for paintings that invoke pop culture, history, and folklore, about his seven-week odyssey to eight Four Seasons properties around the world. "True luxury is in the things you don't notice or see," he continues. As part of his research, he slept, ate, drank, painted, swam, and daydreamed in guest rooms, lobbies, tea lounges, patios, swimming pools, and bars in Florence, Saint Petersburg, Hong Kong, and Punta Mita, to name a few. "Two thousand palm trees have to be trimmed and the leaves removed so that the guest rooms have views of the water," he says of the Punta Mita resort's meticulously maintained gardens, "but you never see anyone doing it because they are gone before guests wake up."

Though he was also privy to whispers of garden-variety indiscretions, what Monreal found most intriguing were those invisible acts of kindness he uncovered. "When a guest had a heart attack at one of the properties and the family never came to visit," he says of an episode he witnessed at one of the hotels during his stay, "the concierge would go every day or send someone in his place to sit with the guest—not because he was asked to do so, but because it was the right thing to do." More notable still, according to Monreal, is that you wouldn't catch anybody within the organization taking credit for this generous human act.

Of course, it isn't very often that a hotel is put to the ultimate bedside manner test. Fortunately, or unfortunately, hospitality is all about first, and seemingly insignificant, impressions. While all great hotel schools and hotel properties share a first commandment—*You only get one shot at a first impression*—few manage to balance a checklist

Following pages: A meal at La Scala in Milan is so stylish and intricately orchestrated that it resembles an opera.

“My kitchen philosophy is knowing the man behind the produce and scouring the markets and Tuscan countryside for independent producers who share my passion for quality. The main value of any dish is the quality of the ingredients. If they have been produced with care, it comes through in the taste.”

Vito Mollica, executive chef and food and beverage director

It's easy to be tempted by perfect produce.

Previous pages: Christian Le Squer, executive chef at Four Seasons Hotel George V in Paris, expertly directs the crafting of a delicious dish. The best hotels are lifestyle canvases that pioneer culinary trends.

SEASONS
TEL

sense of duty with genuine care, consistency with innovation, service with art. As we all know, in order to get to art, you have to break some rules, which requires mastering them in the first place. You also need to have enough confidence in the people to let them riff. "We allow people to authentically be themselves," says O'Sullivan, who brings his background as a poet and artist to the job. "I don't know that other hotel companies would take me!"

To express the Four Seasons ethos, Christian Clerc, president of worldwide hotel operations, says the company's focus for the following pages was on the Artist. "Four Seasons is where excellence meets artistry. These are fifty thousand poets and magicians," he says of the company's employees, "who apply their craft to delight and care for our guests every day."

Sometimes, however, the magic occurs in the tiniest of considerations, like when the housekeeper at Four Seasons Resort Nevis in the West Indies left me a tube of toothpaste, noting that mine had run low, or when my son's stuffed animals were arranged in an artful embrace with his blanket draped behind Elmo like a superhero's cape. Few hotels have the experience and confidence to toggle between the mechanics of service and a warm human hand, and while they might master the former, it's the memory of the much-needed toothpaste that lingers.

Think about when you pull up to a hotel entrance and someone opens your door and offers to take your bag—does it feel truly helpful and fluid or obsequious and rote? When you get to the front desk, do you feel like they are expecting you, or is there lots of keyboard tapping, brow furrowing, and general uncertainty around your reservation? At a mid-level business chain, which is largely automated, a feeling of anonymity is expected—and at times even relished. But at a high-end property, nothing makes you feel less special than having to, say, fill out your e-mail and home addresses, which should already be on file from the many weeks of communication leading up to your arrival. A great hotel, like a good friend, makes you feel like the staff has been waiting for you to arrive so you can all have lunch together.

When you get up to your room, do you get the unnecessary ten-minute tour of the bathroom or the safe? Or does the bellman get straight to a genuinely helpful tutorial on the less obvious room features, such as the iPad that controls the lighting, which might prevent you from frantically searching for light switches and eventually giving up and unplugging the lamp? These minuscule interactions reveal whether a hotel is on autopilot or whether the staff is reading the needs and subtle body language of a guest, who, after a day of travel, is usually screaming for a shower and a nap, stat! One of the most intuitive—and indirectly romantic—gestures I've ever experienced was in a tiny hotel

> "One of the questions I ask myself is, 'What are the guest's expectations the moment they walk into the bar?' Every time, the answer is the same: Treat them the way I would like to be treated. Create the most spectacular experience in a place like no other."

Roberto Altamirano, mixologist

Mixologists astound with their quick and practiced movements, whipping up several impeccable cocktails at once.

Opposite: Armed with encyclopedic knowledge, sommeliers are quick to suggest the perfect pairing for every plate.

Following pages: Fine wines at Four Seasons have been known to defy expectations—and even physics.

PETRVS
1961

in the Yucatán. If you told a staff member what time you wanted your morning coffee delivered to your room, it would appear with a simple knock outside your door. This way you'd get a pot of coffee and two small pastries to get you started without the awkwardness of one of you fumbling for a bathrobe and letting a server into the room while the other buries his or her head under the covers in shame. Room service when on a romantic vacation should feel like an extension of the honeymoon. High-touch service that feels like an interruption ceases to check the "luxury" box. Not having to cover up first thing in the morning is far sexier than any number of rose petals strewn around a bed. And it is when people are at their least self-conscious that they bring the best versions of themselves—and their wardrobes—to the destination and to their relationships.

Why? Because luxury hotels are those fantasy stages that allow you to try on different identities. They are spaces in which you forget what day—and even, in the case of, say, a three-hundred-year-old converted monastery, what century—it is. You have signed up for a level of prescience, sensitivity, and anticipation that you don't get in your normal life. The suspension of time and context inspires risk-taking, giving you permission to finally wear that totally impractical floral-print gown you bought a year ago but that still has its tags,

There's no need for dinner *and* a show—perfectly choreographed room service proves dinner *is* the show.

because somehow it never felt quite right in your regular life. For most people, a great hotel is a safe zone where secrets are kept, a place where nobody knows you never wear floral anything.

As M. Gustave says to his protégé, Zero, "You see, there are still faint glimmers of civilization left in this barbaric slaughterhouse that was once known as humanity. Indeed, that's what we provide in our own modest, humble, insignificant way." Great hotels are microcosms of a place, often representing a city or culture's greatest aspirations for itself. It's no wonder, then, that hotels are the setting in which some of the world's most historic treaties and climate agreements get signed, where coups d'état get hatched, and where cocktails, often drunk to mark such occasions, get invented. The best hotels are lifestyle canvases, incubators of innovation where design and culinary trends make their debuts, and muses that transform cooks into celebrity chefs and decorators into international tastemakers. In their finest hour, "a great hotel like the George V is like haute couture," as Christian Le Squer, the executive chef at the George V in Paris, says, setting a standard of propriety and culture, asking both guests and staff to stand up a little straighter, dress a little better, and be better versions of themselves.

The Clefs d'Or insignia.

Following pages: The Four Seasons private jet takes travelers on customizable whirlwind tours around the globe, from bustling cities to remote islands and everywhere in between.

Pages 38–39: Local poultry enjoy a luxury lifestyle, as if they were guests themselves.

FOUR
SEASONS
Clefs d'Or

★ ★ ★ ★ ★

FOUR SEAS

ONS

"Flowers are an integral part of a hotel. People feel at home, they feel comforted, they feel a sense of luxury. They think, 'If the first thing I see is flowers when I enter this hotel, I can't wait to see what happens when I get to my room!'"

Jeff Leatham, artistic director and florist extraordinaire

Celebrity florist Jeff Leatham and his lavish arrangements, including his famous tilted flowers, are signatures of the chic lobby at the George V.

Previous pages: (left) Gardeners cultivate the flowers and plants across each property on a microscopic level, making sure each petal and blade of grass is immaculate and accounted for. *(right)* Artists are the masters behind all the creative flourishes that adorn each hotel.

“We express our love for service with flawless execution rather than words. It is through the efforts of many passionate individuals and their unstinting dedication that unparalleled experiences are delivered to our guests.”

Antoine Chahwan, regional vice president and general manager

Housekeepers appear with anything a guest might need, taking note of guest preferences for future visits and leaving only spotless rooms with gleaming surfaces in their wake.

"Our modern chalets in the heart of the French Alps build on the unrivaled resort experience created by the Rothschild family nearly a century ago. Today, we celebrate this heritage by connecting with our guests to create positive impressions that last a lifetime."

Sandrine Lobet, hotel ambassador

There's no better place to experience
the French Alps than Four Seasons Hotel Megève.

Following pages: With its evocative design, The Surf Club is a home or studio
away from home that inspires creative types.

“Four Seasons is all about emotion, about belonging, about being proud to contribute to something special as a team.”

Silke Maulick, director of housekeeping

Outside, Paris and its treasures; inside, a well-appointed suite waiting to welcome an explorer home for the night.

Previous pages: The dreamlike view of Victoria Harbour through the floor-to-ceiling windows at Four Seasons Hotel Hong Kong provides an indelible memory for guests.

Following pages: Staff members cast a wide net to catch the freshest of everything.

Pages 56–57: Mixologists' creations are often inspired by local traditions and recipes.

> “Mix a heart full of passion with genuine kindness, shake it vigorously with creativity, and let guests sip the most memorable experience of their lives.”

Sophie Larrouture, mixologist

FOUR SEASONS

Spas are temples of wellness that offer guests tranquil settings to find balance after a day of adventure.

Previous pages: Handling all tasks with both pride and elegance is the Four Seasons way.

Following pages: Ideal weather conditions and a practiced swing ensure no experience is ever a bogey.

WIND
2 m
100%
LOW
NICE
HIGH
20%

456
2

Mixologists perfect every ingredient.

Following pages: Millennials are the future for the multigenerational families who find happiness at Four Seasons.

FOUR SEASONS
FOUR SEASONS
FOUR SEASONS

“I try to give the staff a sense of belonging. Like a conductor, I find the right part for each employee in order to achieve perfect harmony.”

Patrizio Cipollini, general manager

General managers, including Patrizio Cipollini in Florence, are maestros who conduct their teams to provide excellent service, since true luxury has everything to do with people.

Previous pages: At every property, a new adventure awaits.

Following pages: Four Seasons is constantly redefining and elevating the meaning of service, delivering anything a modern guest—and her entourage—may need.

"A three-star chef is like a fashion designer or a great perfumer looking for new scents. My passion is to give and to share, as if my guests were coming for lunch or dinner in my home. I don't work *at* Four Seasons Hotel George V, but rather *for* the happiness of the customers."

Christian Le Squer, executive chef

Christian Le Squer has received three Michelin stars and shows the ultimate precision and control in working directly with each of the ingredients in his recipes.

Previous pages: A guest wholeheartedly ready to experience a culinary journey.

le cinq
chef Christian Le - Squer

Even vegetable gardens are prizeworthy at Four Seasons.

“Nothing is impossible for the crew of invisible warriors. You let us know, we make it happen. You don’t let us know, we figure it out and still make it happen.”

Beata Lajos, director of housekeeping

Guest rooms are visions of fantasy.

“It is our unique formula that makes Four Seasons irresistible: self-esteem, empathy, and a passion for excellence.”

Felix Murillo, general manager

Housekeeping is impeccable and beyond one's wildest dreams.

Following pages: Creature comforts in each suite enhance the guest experience.

“Engaging the whole person is the key to strong culture, and sometimes that means making time to have a little giggle.”

Aziza Ali, operational learning and development manager

Even stately statues take time to indulge their playful side.

Following pages: Four Seasons' expert concoctions elevate drinks to an art form.

Guests can let their imaginations run wild at this rooftop pool at Four Seasons Hotel Dubai International Financial Centre.

A dramatic infinity pool in Hong Kong welcomes playful competition.

Following pages: Some settings require no adornment.

Caprice restaurant, the recipient of two Michelin stars, is also the site of an expansive cellar housing Hong Kong's widest selection of artisanal cheeses.

"Making the best cheese is an art. Small-batch craftsmen create cheeses of deep complexity, each one with a story behind it."

Stéphane Rabot, restaurant director

“Interaction is one of the most beautiful things that you can do to add positivity to others’ lives, at the same time enhancing your own. When I do good things for others, I move the energy within them and within myself. Four Seasons gives me this opportunity every single day.”

Wdson Brum, senior spa director

Each Four Seasons staff member brings his or her own personality and interests to the mix, creating a vibrant team. Wdson Brum, director of the Luceo Spa at Lion Palace in Saint Petersburg, goes searching for displaced birds that he releases back into their habitats.

Following pages: Each property goes above and beyond in its own way to offer diners a proper good-morning greeting.

Gardeners tend to the landscape to ensure a beautiful view from each room.

Unconventional experiences are a Four Seasons signature.

“Everything is calm and wonderful under the sea; I’m so lucky this is my job. I have the opportunity to experience a whole other world most people don’t see, and I’m excited when I can introduce newcomers to the wonders of the ocean.”

Abdul Latheef, assistant dive manager

Abdul Latheef brings guests on a tour through an underwater paradise.

Staff members never run out of ways to astonish.

At Four Seasons, all beings can enjoy the good life.

Four Seasons goes to great lengths to give guests their "perfect catch" moment.

"Beautiful buildings are a stage on which our employees perform their art every day."

Christian Clerc, president of worldwide hotel operations

Housekeepers are like saints when it comes to exceeding guest expectations.

Following pages: While Voavah is a remote island in the Maldives, it is still well within the realm of Four Seasons' excellent service.

"What makes Four Seasons inspiring is its ability to allow people to be their authentic selves. Rules are guidelines that can and should be broken if they deter from this goal."

John O'Sullivan, regional vice president and general manager

Cesar "El Anfibio" brings service directly to swimming guests for maximum pool enjoyment.

Following pages: (left) Master yogi Andrew Sealy's classes challenge guests to reach new heights. *(right)* Turtles hatch and return to the sea on a beach in Punta Mita. The resort donates both time and money to preserving wildlife, a cause that resonates with even its youngest guests.

There is no end to the experts and specialists who work to enhance the guest experience, including the falconer who makes weekly visits to Four Seasons Resort Punta Mita.

Voavah, available to rent out privately, is pleasantly secluded, though guests are always eager to tag their dazzling location.

Anything is possible during a stay at Four Seasons—guests' wishes should reach to infinity.

Following pages: (left) The hotels are a melting pot of culture, embracing a multitude of traditions to make each guest feel his or her best. *(right)* Guests of Peacock Alley, a historic loggia at The Surf Club, have included Frank Sinatra, Elizabeth Taylor, and Winston Churchill.

An artful dish at Le Sirenuse restaurant by Antonio Mermolia, executive chef at The Surf Club.

“We all have gifts, and I am fortunate that Four Seasons has given me a space to share mine.”

Ryan Hennessy, astronomer

Sunsets are to be eternalized, on or off camera.

"Real people come here to feel like celebrities, and celebrities come to feel like real people."

Mark Warren, Jr., guest relations assistant manager

Mark Warren, Jr., offers service with a smile even over the phone.

“Excellence is never an accident.”

Victoria Ivanova, hotel ambassador

Room service presents the catch of the day.

Following pages: Hotel happiness often depends more on the many little things you don't see than on the few you do.

“The real magic lies in the deep-rootedness of our approach: Guests feel the same cohesion when they walk into any one of our properties. Four Seasons is like a security blanket for travelers.”

Armando Kraenzlin, regional vice president and general manager

Every stay empowers guests to go beyond the traditional and leap straight into the unconventional.

Following pages: The lawn in Florence hosts some flamboyant visitors.

"The success of our hotels is deeply linked to our exceptional culture, which revolves around our people, an obsessive attention to detail, and exceeding our guests' expectations. We focus on providing unique experiences that reflect the heart and soul of a destination."

Jean Claude Wietzel, regional vice president and general manager

La Cave, the wine cellar at George V, is the site from which the stone used to build the Arc de Triomphe was extracted in the early 1800s.

Following pages: Dining among La Cave's unparalleled collection of vintages is every oenophile's dream.

La Cave

“Wine is the root of hedonism at this hotel.”

Eric Beaumard, restaurant director

Eric Beaumard is the gatekeeper of 50,000 bottles in Paris. The property's wine vault, La Cave, is as secure as Fort Knox.

Following pages: (left) Chef Antonio Mermolia brings an authentic dose of his native Italy to Florida.
(right) No presentation is too extravagant for a fine wine.

"When the art of beauty and the science of human-centered functionality intersect, there lies the power of perfect design."

Dana Kalczak, vice president of design

Frescoes on the ceiling at Four Seasons Hotel Firenze—which was the private residence of Florentine nobles for centuries—come alive with history, letting guests see through the eyes of Michelangelo, da Vinci, and beyond.

Following pages: The regal entrance of Four Seasons Hotel Lion Palace in Saint Petersburg, whose lions were immortalized in Alexander Pushkin's 1833 poem "The Bronze Horseman," is fit for a visit from Cinderella.

FOUR SEASONS

FOUR SEASONS

"I see service through two words: connection and empathy. What you remember after any experience is how someone made you feel."

Estreya Gosalbez, hotel manager

Remembering each guest goes a long way toward creating lifelong connections.

Previous pages: (left) Picture yourself enjoying a private bacchanalian feast. *(right)* A mischievous guest dances to his own tune with a party in his suite.

Each day, Four Seasons writes a new chapter in hospitality history.

Following pages: The kissing spot in Florence is a favorite of honeymooning couples and even the occasional pair of birds in spring!

Each property's artwork and decor evolve with the times.
To get to art, you have to break rules, which requires mastering them in the first place.

Following pages: (left) Dionysus joins in enjoying the bounty of Four Seasons.
(right) Discerning guests appreciate the delectable taste of homegrown ingredients.

4S

“My deep passion for cuisine began a long time ago with my family in the south of Italy. We genuinely love making people happy by taking care of their meals. What makes me happiest is hearing from my guests that they love the food. That motivates me to be even better the next day and to feel like anything is possible!”

Antonio Mermolia, executive chef

A passion for satisfying diners is the most important ingredient in any dish.

Following pages: Anyone would say "I do" to such a splendid display!

Say Si

XXX

“It’s about moments: the moment a guest enters their room or the lobby for the first time, the moment a server remembers their favorite dessert or personalizes a birthday cake. It’s the moments we create that last forever.”

Christopher Ford, executive pastry chef

All birthdays should be celebrated with gusto.

“What drives me each day is that I am the first impression for our guests, and I love seeing the glimmer in their eyes as they arrive. I have developed many relationships with repeat guests over the years, and it is so fulfilling to meet their children or even their grandchildren.”

John Tyler, bellman

Bellmen are glad to take care of furry friends—a happy pet makes a happy owner!

Following pages: Advances in technology bring upgrades in the level of service concierges are able to achieve without ever losing the human touch.

"The best parts are those unscripted moments when acts of kindness surprise and delight our guests and reaffirm that making people feel special is simply priceless."

Yvette Thomas-Henry, general manager

A young celebrity makes her exit.

“Four Seasons allows not only our guests but also every member of the team to feel welcome and at home.”

Alizée Flores, receptionist

Even the most un-expected guests are made to feel as though the hotel has been waiting just for them. After all, hospitality is about first impressions.

Following pages: (left) Colorful humor is always a welcome ingredient.
(right) Local birds hope to discover the secret of the Fountain of Youth at the spa in Punta Mita.

“My approach to service is easy: I listen with my heart and I treat everyone with as much importance as I would my own children. My passion is to spread to the world that we are our own healers.”

Shoshana Weinberg, senior director of spa

Shoshana Weinberg, the star of the Hong Kong spa, is known by many names, among them director of wellness, wise woman, moon sister, and herbalist.

"Make a difference each day with those who cross your path in your journey. That's what hospitality is."

Uday Rao, general manager

Guests are always welcome to come as they are.

Following pages: A bonsai tree depicts the four seasons.

G

H

"Many guests choose spa treatments based on what is familiar, but we tailor services based on what will be most beneficial to each individual so that we can make a genuine difference."

Dr. Shylesh Subramanya, spa director

A caviar facial is the pinnacle of luxury.

Following pages: A plate from L'Orangerie, with knives crafted by a master Japanese artisan that show off an all-but-lost tradition of fine blade-making.

“Like wine, great service is all about balance: balancing professionalism, authenticity, and attentiveness. With the right balance, we create personalized experiences that yield long-lasting memories for our guests.”

Yann Hangouet, head sommelier

Sommeliers taste each wine to ensure they can describe all its nuances when recommending pairings.

Previous pages: (left) Anna Wong, catering director in Hong Kong, curates every detail of guests' gatherings so they can focus on creating unforgettable memories. *(right)* Chef Yan Tak, the world's first Chinese Michelin-starred chef, serves exclusively exquisite, prize-winning dim sum *(shown following pages)*.

Pages 200–201: From exquisite interiors that marry form and function to views and vistas that inspire the imagination, there is always more than meets the eye at Four Seasons.

1979
RICHEBOURG
GRAND CRU
Henry Jayer

> "It's all about the details, looking at everything with a sharp eye and not accepting something because it may be easier, and never, ever saying no. Something is always possible."

Javier Loureiro, director of guest experience

The Four Seasons private jet has the amenities of a hotel, including five-star dining and dedicated concierge service, with the added benefit of being able to travel the world.

Previous pages: Nature entertains guests aboard the hotel's private yacht.

1285
FOUR SEASONS

"Hospitality has no frontiers, just like our employees' willingness to make our guests feel at home, wherever they may travel from."

Mary Hapner, executive assistant to the general manager

Four Seasons properties are global embassies where any traveler can find something familiar and feel at home, no matter their point of origin.

FOUR SEASONS
concierge
4
SEASONS

In 1961, Isadore Sharp conceived of the first dream of Four Seasons with a hotel in Toronto, Canada. Today, this dream continues to grow as the company emphasizes the excellence and talent in each of the people who join its team.

Sets of room keys evoke the Clefs d'Or emblem proudly worn by first-class concierges.

FOUR SEASONS CONTRIBUTORS

Abdul Latheef, assistant dive manager, Four Seasons Resort Maldives at Landaa Giraavaru

Alizée Flores, receptionist, Four Seasons Hotel Buenos Aires

Andrew Sealy, yoga instructor, Four Seasons Hotel Los Angeles at Beverly Hills

Anna Wong, director of catering, Four Seasons Hotel Hong Kong

Antoine Chahwan, regional vice president and general manager, Four Seasons Hotel Singapore

Antonio Mermolia, executive chef, Four Seasons Hotel at The Surf Club, Surfside, Florida

Armando Kraenzlin, regional vice president and general manager, Four Seasons Resort Maldives at Landaa Giraavaru

Aziza Ali, operational learning and development manager, Four Seasons Resort Orlando at Walt Disney World Resort

Beata Lajos, director of housekeeping, Grand-Hôtel du Cap-Ferrat, A Four Seasons Hotel

Chan Yan Tak, executive Chinese chef, Four Seasons Hotel Hong Kong

Christian Clerc, president of worldwide hotel operations, Four Seasons Hotels and Resorts

Christian Le Squer, executive chef, Four Seasons Hotel George V, Paris

Christopher Ford, executive pastry chef, Beverly Wilshire, A Four Seasons Hotel

Dana Kalczak, vice president of design, Four Seasons Hotels and Resorts

Dickson Cheng, guest services manager, Four Seasons Hotel Singapore

Eric Beaumard, restaurant director, Four Seasons Hotel George V, Paris

Estreya Gosalbez, hotel manager, Four Seasons Hotel Atlanta

Felix Murillo, general manager, Four Seasons Hotel Lion Palace Saint Petersburg

Isadore Sharp, founder and chairman, Four Seasons Hotels and Resorts

Javier Loureiro, director of guest experience, Four Seasons Private Jet

Jean Claude Wietzel, regional vice president and general manager, Four Seasons Hotel George V, Paris

Jeff Leatham, artistic director and florist extraordinaire, Four Seasons Hotel George V, Paris

John O'Sullivan, regional vice president and general manager, Four Seasons Resort Punta Mita

John Tyler, bellman, Four Seasons Hotel Chicago

Mark Warren, Jr., guest relations assistant manager, Four Seasons Hotel at The Surf Club, Surfside, Florida

Mary Hapner, executive assistant to the general manager, Four Seasons Hotel Washington, D.C.

Patrizio Cipollini, general manager, Four Seasons Hotel Firenze

Roberto Altamirano, mixologist, Four Seasons Resort Costa Rica

Ryan Hennessy, astronomer, Four Seasons Resort Jackson Hole

Sandrine Lobet, hotel ambassador, Four Seasons Hotel Megève

Shoshana Weinberg, senior director of spa, Four Seasons Hotel Hong Kong

Dr. Shylesh Subramanya, spa director, Four Seasons Resort Maldives at Landaa Giraavaru

Silke Maulick, director of housekeeping, Four Seasons Hotel George V, Paris

Sophie Larrouture, mixologist, Four Seasons Hotel des Bergues Geneva

Stéphane Rabot, restaurant director, Caprice, Four Seasons Hotel Hong Kong

Uday Rao, general manager, Four Seasons Resorts Bali at Sayan and Jimbaran Bay

Victoria Ivanova, hotel ambassador, Four Seasons Hotel George V, Paris

Vito Mollica, executive chef and food and beverage director, Four Seasons Hotel Firenze

Wdson Brum, senior spa director, Four Seasons Hotel Lion Palace Saint Petersburg

Yann Hangouet, head sommelier, Four Seasons Hotel des Bergues Geneva

Yvette Thomas-Henry, general manager, Four Seasons Hotel Atlanta

ACKNOWLEDGMENTS

Assouline would like to thank Four Seasons and its wonderful employees for their contribution to this book—they make this company special. Thank you to Ignasi Monreal, Sonia Adamczak, and Pilar Guzmán for their wonderful collaboration.

Assouline Publishing
3 Park Avenue, 27th floor
New York, NY 10016 USA
Tel: 212-989-6769 Fax: 212-647-0005
www.assouline.com

Editorial direction: Esther Kremer
Art direction: Jihyun Kim
Editor: Lindsey Tulloch

ISBN: 9781614287117

Printed in Italy.